EVERYTHING YOU KNOW ABOUT ORGANIZATIONAL BEHAVIOR YOU LEARNED IN HIGH SCHOOL

VICTOR P. BECKER

Copyright © 2019 Victor P. Becker.

All rights reserved. No part of this book may be used or reproduced by any means, graphic, electronic, or mechanical, including photocopying, recording, taping or by any information storage retrieval system without the written permission of the author except in the case of brief quotations embodied in critical articles and reviews.

Archway Publishing books may be ordered through booksellers or by contacting:

Archway Publishing
1663 Liberty Drive
Bloomington, IN 47403
www.archwaypublishing.com
1 (888) 242-5904

Because of the dynamic nature of the Internet, any web addresses or links contained in this book may have changed since publication and may no longer be valid. The views expressed in this work are solely those of the author and do not necessarily reflect the views of the publisher, and the publisher hereby disclaims any responsibility for them.

Any people depicted in stock imagery provided by Getty Images are models, and such images are being used for illustrative purposes only. Certain stock imagery © Getty Images.

ISBN: 978-1-4808-7934-8 (sc)
ISBN: 978-1-4808-7932-4 (hc)
ISBN: 978-1-4808-7933-1 (e)

Library of Congress Control Number: 2019908127

Print information available on the last page.

Archway Publishing rev. date: 07/08/2019

For Andrew and Bennett.

CONTENTS

Introduction ix
1 The Cool Kids and the Inner Circle 1
2 Got to Get That Varsity Letter: Title Is
  Everything 11
3 Report Cards and the Cirque du Performance
  Appraisal 19
4 Superlatives and Employee Recognition 31
5 Leadership 37
6 Where am I Supposed to Sit? 49
7 The Power of Teams 59
8 Yakety-Yak 67
9 Bullies and Predators 77
10 Friendships and Work Relationships 83
11 Final Examination 93
About the Author 97

INTRODUCTION

During my more than thirty-five years of experience as a human resources professional in large, midsize, and small companies I have had the good fortune to be associated with many phenomenal individuals who were great role models, teachers, mentors, and peers. I've had a front-row seat observing people and their behavior patterns in the workplace. Upon reflection, I realized that companies are successful in spite of their unrecognized organizational dysfunction. Organizational behavior, at all levels, can be best defined as adolescent, and the behavior patterns within the business environment are deeply rooted in the volatile period of our high school years. In other words, our behavior as adults in the workplace is eerily similar to the individual and group dynamics that we experienced as teenagers.

Remember—the universe is in a constant state of flux. Behavior patterns that occur routinely in an environment such as high school should evolve as the environment changes. Logically, new behavior patterns should develop. My hypothesis is that new behavior patterns did not develop as the environment shifted to a business environment. In my opinion, the patterns became even more extreme. Why did this happen? I do not have a clue, and I believe there are people much smarter than me who will be able to peel the layers of that onion. I will focus on the what by describing core examples of the high school experience and drawing comparisons to the business environment.

For many of us, our teenage years are probably the most unsettling of our lives. We were not sure where we fit in. Our future was a big chasm or black hole of the unknown. We applied so much pressure on ourselves to have answers when we did not really even understand the questions. Our lives were a *hot mess*. However, this was not a bad thing, because it actually set the stage in preparing us for the complex, interpersonal relationships that we must navigate in order to get ahead—whatever that means.

Everything You Know about Organizational Behavior You Learned in High School is an easy-to-read guide in practical management development leadership. It's intended to assist business leaders and human resources professionals in identifying and correcting adolescent organizational behaviors on the job. Through humorous and relatable stories drawn from my experiences, we will examine the organizational dysfunction in the context of real challenges in areas such as employee recognition, performance management, leadership, predators and bullies, the power of teams, and more. "Simple fixes" are offered for each area.

The good news is that everything we experience in high school is great preparation for what we will face as adults in the business world. The bad news is that nothing changes in the business world because, in my opinion, our behavior as adult professionals is no different than it was back in high school. We are trapped in the *Twilight Zone*. Did we really graduate from high school? Academically yes. Behaviorally? No ... heck *no*.

Success in any business is difficult to achieve. Competition is fierce, especially in the global arena, and establishing a competitive edge is oftentimes the difference between thriving and surviving. The margin is very thin. Organizations that can function quickly and efficiently will win the day every time. In order to do so, we must leave high school behaviors in the rearview mirror and become the adult in the room. Capitalize on the insights offered while relating though your own experiences in order to lead your organization forward. Let's get to work.

1

The Cool Kids and the Inner Circle

As a career human resources professional, I was afforded the opportunity to closely observe people and their behavior in the workplace. I am not a psychologist. I will present my observations and conclusions from a layperson's perspective.

Human nature is fascinating! Once understood, if understanding is possible, most actions are fairly predictable given a constant set of circumstances. For example, a group of highly creative individuals who are micromanaged will eventually rebel. My responsibility as a human resources professional is to recognize the behavioral patterns arising from basic human nature, proactively prevent the rebellion, and move the individuals involved to a win-win outcome.

Here's an interesting example because it seems to be somewhat contradictory. High performers are driven by a fear of failure and, consequently, always believe they can or should be working harder and doing more. They are rarely satisfied. The human resources function must assuage this anxiety by providing the proper incentive rewards and recognition vehicles in order to retain these key contributors.

Conversely, midlevel and average performers feel that they are doing what is expected of them—no more and no less. They are satisfied with their levels of contribution and will generally never push the envelope to perform at a higher level. These steady performers represent the largest portion of workers in an organization, and the human resources role is to encourage this group to perform at a higher level without pressuring to the point that these steady Eddies and Edwinas fear that their jobs are in jeopardy. It is a delicate balancing act.

Many individuals espouse the premise that people behave differently in the workplace than they do outside work. While this viewpoint may have merit at a task level or in communication style, it has been my experience that people have the same needs, desires, and behavior patterns in both environments. Everyone, no matter what the environment, wants to be cool and popular as well as respected, appreciated, and recognized for his or her contributions and achievements. We will examine all of these characteristics in the chapters that follow. So let's begin with the cool kids.

There is always a group of individuals that everyone acknowledges is cool. In 2014 the musical group Echosmith, from Chino, California, released the single

"Cool Kids." The song symbolically describes the internal conflict that many teenagers experience in trying to find their places in society. Echosmith has poignantly captured the group dynamic that we have all experienced. We all want to be cool.

According to the website www.urbandictionary.com, cool is popular, like in a social hierarchy, which is described as a system or organization in which people or groups are ranked one above the other according to status or authorities.

Popularity is an extraordinary phenomenon. We all desire to be popular. It is a status that is easy to understand but difficult to define. How is it manifested and measured? Is there a point or an event that indicates that you are now popular? It is clearly a subjective perception of what appears to be commonly accepted by many people.

I believe there are two distinctions that warrant consideration in describing popularity and being a cool kid. They are the *trendsetter* and the *follower*. Trendsetters march to the beat of different drums and really do not care what other people think. In most cases, these individuals tend to act on their own desires. In high school, this is best illustrated by elements such as fashion statements, recreational activities, and music. Trendsetters are generally considered cool kids unless they are so eccentric that they are isolated. On the other hand, the cool-kid trendsetter is unique yet inspires others to follow. The cool kids are always popular. The cool kids are the high school power brokers.

Followers aren't sure what they really want or how they should act or with whom they should hang out. They care about what everyone thinks, which is probably why they are undecided. As a result, they fall in line with the behavior of the group that is believed to be at the top of the social hierarchy. Followers realize that this approach has some risk because they might choose the wrong group. There are many groups to choose from, and we will examine that in more detail later. For now, suffice it to say followers feel comfortable at the moment that they are on the path to popularity and coolness.

Unfortunately, as teenagers, most of us did not have much game. Our attempts to break into the coolness realm were often awkward, clumsy, and ineffective. No matter how hard we tried to belong by doing silly things like wearing the fashionable clothes of the day or name-dropping our access to a local celebrity or that the star quarterback lived next door, success was not an option. The follower might become popular but never becomes a cool kid.

As adults, we still want to be like the cool kids. The old feelings and insecurities come rushing back, shaking our confidence as they did before. The goal is identical. However, the methodology differs slightly. In high school, we wanted to belong to the club so desperately that we realized, probably for the first time in our lives, that it was acceptable to compromise our individuality and, to a lesser degree, our integrity, to achieve that objective. The end justified the means. We began to develop our prowess in the art of kissing ass. My use of the phrase probably makes you cringe a bit as your mind races to the literal activity. However, this method of getting what you want is, more often than not, successful in organizations around the world.

Kissing Ass

How does ass kissing work? What techniques are tried and true? What environment is most conducive to it? At which organizational levels is it most successful? These are all excellent questions, and there are a variety of responses depending on the type of industry, company size, and organizational structure. However, my primary goal is to keep this narrative basic. Fortunately or unfortunately, since the majority of my career was in high technology, my examples will have a technology slant.

In most cases, ass-kissing environments evolve surreptitiously. Every organization experiences some form of political activity. Getting things done requires compromise and a healthy give-and-take. It requires broad access to decision makers and influence peddlers throughout the organization. For the upwardly hopefuls, it is critical to see and be seen at work-sponsored social events in order to demonstrate the ability and stamina to hang with the big dogs. Herein lies the genesis of the ass-kissing environment.

In organizations, the cool kids are those individuals with the power and authority to affect careers, compensation, work assignments, and organizational culture. These people are found primarily in the executive suite; however, additional VIPs reside lower in the hierarchy. The cool kids are the power brokers: they set the tone and priorities; they drive the pace; and they create the culture of the organization—ergo, the ass-kissing environment.

Just as in high school, we want to be like the cool kids. In the business world, this can occur in a couple of ways. The first is the more difficult: the upwardly hopefuls must establish themselves as people the cool kids rely on. These are generally individuals in pure executive-staff roles or executive administrators. They often become gatekeepers to the cool kids, and therefore, they become junior cool kids because of their ability to control access. The second is more obvious: to be promoted into the club. For the upwardly hopefuls, this is the most secure method because their new roles with their new, wicked-cool titles assure that they are now members. But there is no guarantee that a promoted upwardly hopeful will be embraced as a cool kid; this is because of the inner-circle effect.

The Inner Circle

An integral part of the clique is the mysterious inner circle. Every organization or management team has a small number of individuals whom the leader trusts more for their counsel than the broader group of direct reports. This is natural and in and of itself not a bad thing. The inner circle can develop into a disruptive and divisive entity if it is utilized as an exclusive club with privileges for those in it. This has exactly the same effect as the cool-kids scenario. Let me share a more impactful example.

Many executives tend to manage by a set of objectives established at the beginning of the fiscal year. Oftentimes these objectives are long on strategic vision, growth, and market dominance but short on realistic execution plans. These objectives are well packaged in a PowerPoint slide deck, with all the graphs and effects that is rolled out to the management team for cascading communication throughout the organization. This is where the fun begins, because each functional organization receives its marching orders and charges ahead to achieve the objectives. The organizational silos are in full operation as there is often conflict between the organizations to accomplish the goals. As an example, the sales organization has an objective to increase revenues by 25 percent year over year. They can accomplish this goal only by launching a new product in the first quarter of the year so that the ninety-day selling cycle will allow time to generate the necessary deals to achieve the number. The finance organization must reduce headcount by 10 percent by the end of the second quarter in order to meet the financial earnings-per-share guidance announced. Yet headcount reductions that would presumably be implemented in research and development, product management, and marketing would seriously affect the new product launch. Something has to give. This is where the ass-kissing accelerates into overdrive.

The executives recognize the conundrum and solicit input and recommendations from their direct reports. In my experience, very few executives approached problems with a totally open mind. They have a preconceived outcome in mind and want to validate that outcome or discover a big gotcha from out of nowhere. They are actually searching for individuals who will tell them what they want to hear as well as serving the best interest of their own function, oftentimes at the expense of other functions. Where are these individuals who will tell them what they want to hear? *Bingo*! You guessed it: *the inner circle*! This is ass kissing at the most advanced level. As long as individuals are rewarded and supported for this behavior, it will continue unabated and proliferate throughout the organization like a virus.

Vic's Fix

- ☐ Utilize the inner circle as a management tool, not a weapon.
- ☐ Establish three to four achievable objectives that are properly vetted and linked across organizational lines so that the functions work together where success is defined as a team win.
- ☐ Approach decisions with an open mind; *seek out conflicting opinions;* leave your ego at home—there is no place for it in the office.
- ☐ Hold people accountable for their performance and the manner in which they perform.
- ☐ *Just say no* to ass kissers!

2

Got to Get That Varsity Letter: Title Is Everything

I guess the place to begin on this aspect of behavior is with the desire that we all share to be acknowledged as an important and impactful person. In the high school hierarchy, this has its challenges.

In a four-year program, you enter high school as a freshman around age fourteen. You are basically as relevant as a paramecium. If you are a young man, your face has not caught up with your nose. You maintain a six-month supply of acne medicine, and the topper is that you have absolutely zero coolness. The young women entering high school generally have a better edge than their male counterparts. They are generally at least two years ahead on the emotional maturity scale. They are, however, still in the freshman class and are basically nonentities.

Things get a little better in sophomore year, primarily because there is now a class of freshman beneath you. Some of the more gifted sophomores may have an opportunity to earn that varsity Letter. But generally, these opportunities are attainable when you become a junior and enter the realm of the upper class. As upperclassmen and women, you rule the school. When you make varsity anything, you probably earn your letter or jacket by the end of first semester. You have arrived with the symbol of validation for all to see and marvel at—ta-da! To be clear, this does not necessarily mean that you are now a cool kid, though you do have more street cred than the average non-letter jacket–wearing student. You are now at least a VIP because you have the jacket or the symbol of being important. You proudly wear that jacket no matter what the weather or temperature because that jacket defines you.

As an interesting life lesson, I learned that as important as that jacket was to me in high school, it became a pariah in college. If you wore the symbol of your high school glory days on campus, you were jeered mercilessly by fellow collegians. I packed the jacket away. My mom ended up wearing it for quite a number of years. It was a good lesson about looking forward and not getting stuck in the past.

In the business environment, the same desire to be acknowledged as an important and impactful person still exists because title is everything. It is your metaphorical varsity letter jacket, your symbol of importance. The similarities to the structure outlined above are remarkable. I think you will see what I mean.

One of the primary responsibilities of the human resources function is to monitor job roles/functions and compensation levels in order to remain fair and competitive in the marketplace. It is important to know that a software developer with certain education and experience or skills should be paid at market salary level. Adjustments are required at times to maintain the competitive positioning of your workforce. It is a tedious process. I will stay at fifty thousand feet with the hope of keeping you awake!

There are basically two job tracks or career paths, the individual contributor track and the management track. The titling scheme for the individual contributor track is extraordinarily similar to the four-year structure in high school. The levels incorporate ranges of education and experience necessary to be categorized at the particular level. I will utilize the software development path as an example:

Software Career Development Path

INDIVIDUAL CONTRIBUTOR TRACK	MANAGEMENT TRACK
• Associate Software Developer	• Manager, Software Development
• Software Developer	• Director, Software Development
• Senior Software Developer	• Senior Director, R&D
• Lead Software Developer	• Vice President, R&D

Software Development Benchmark Titles

The Allure of Titles

As mentioned, maintaining job titles and levels is an important part of the human resources (HR) function. It not only forms the basis for competitive leveling in the external arena, it is also the foundation for internal equity within the company. It seems like a pretty straightforward exercise in that the majority of organizations have a great deal of roles, titles, and functions that are good matches. In the HR trade, these are referred to as benchmark jobs (titles) and are the basis for the external market place comparisons.

This is a disciplined process, and the results are determined through the collection and summarization of sound empirical information. For the most part, people accept their title assignments and understand how the titles were established. However, for many individuals the title is negotiable, and in order to obtain the best one possible, they are always negotiating, because title is everything. The title determines your compensation level, your level of decision-making authority, your influence, and your validation that you are an important individual. The upwardly hopefuls will constantly push an agenda for the highest title attainable with the lowest requirements possible. Welcome back to Thomas A. Edison High School.

Human resources professionals deal with many serious employee relations issues such as discrimination, harassment, substance abuse, and bullying. Though I have to declare that I have spent many more cycles with executives, managers, and employees regarding the determination of the right title "for an individual in a totally unique role that does not really fit our structure." Seriously?

Do you suspect that the majority of these discussions involved members of the inner circle or junior inner circle? *You betcha*! Just for giggles and grins, let me share some arguments presented to me over the course of my career as someone sought to justify a bigger or higher level title than was warranted.

Blast from My Past

- Executive: "He has been doing the same work for the past four years and has done an okay job. He deserves to be promoted to the next level, otherwise we are going to lose him. He's a really good guy, and he is the shortstop on the softball team!"

Believe it or not, he said it with a straight face and did not even realize that I played second base on the softball team. I knew the shortstop well. He often discussed his job and how much he enjoyed his situation, work hours, etc. He viewed it as a lifestyle role and had zero desire for additional responsibility. *Denied!* The individual remained with the organization in the same role for the next eight years until the company was acquired, and then he lost his job as a result of the acquisition.

- Director: "As part of the recent reorganization, I now report directly to the senior vice president, services. I need to be a vice president in order to have the credibility and respect of the other direct reports on the staff."

  Are you kidding me? This is one of the more common pleas in that there is some urban legend in companies where it is believed that your title is determined by the title of the individual you report to and the bigger title is necessary to make you effective. It is the person, not the title, that earns the respect. The reporting structure should never dictate title. What is the job, and how is it leveled in the benchmark?

- Individual Contributor: "I am going to my first trade show. I am certain that I will be making many new contacts, and I need to be able to present people with a business card with a title that will impress them."

I had to be honest and direct when I replied, "If *you* do not impress them, you will never get the opportunity to give them your business card, so whatever title is on the card is irrelevant. On the other hand, if *you* are impressive and get the opportunity to present your card, the only thing that will be important is your contact info. The title does not mean diddly-squat!

Vic's Fix

- Assign titles based on the role, its requirements, and its match to the market. Assigning titles in any other way will make it difficult to maintain any semblance of internal equity or market competitiveness.
- Avoid unique "onesie" roles that are totally designed for an individual. In the rare circumstances where these roles are required, utilize generic, innocuous titles such as "special projects," "executive staff," "special assignment," "interim," or "acting capacity."
- Never use a title as a counteroffer measure. It never works in the long term because whatever the reason that caused the individual to consider leaving in the first place probably has not changed.

- Maintain good discipline regarding business cards and titles. The business card title and the official title should be identical. Trouble starts when the titles vary.

3

Report Cards and the Cirque du Performance Appraisal

Report cards or progress reports are grades. Once you enter high school, grades become the key to your future, especially if you are bound for college. Grades determine if you participate in extracurricular activities such as sports, band, cheerleading, etc. Grades are a critical component in college admissions and scholarship awards. So yes, grades are an important aspect of what happens in high school and beyond.

In my high school, we received report cards four times per year. On the report card, you received an achievement grade as well as an effort mark for each class from the teacher of that class. (Hold on to this fact for a challenge later.) The grades were the normal grades that drove a GPA (4.0 = A; 3.5 = B+ etc.) and the effort marks were 1 – you are practically perfect; 2 – c'mon, butthead, you can do better; 3 – you suck.

Now, I am not sure how this played out in all schools, but our report cards were handed to us in homeroom, and we had one week to bring them back in signed by a parent. We generally received them on a Thursday or Friday for reasons that, I believe to this day, were intended to ruin our weekend.

The fascinating part of this drama was that my parents focused more on the effort mark than the achievement grade. What is that all about? I have been a "bottom line" person for as long as I can remember. I never accepted the whine, "It's not whether you win or lose but how you play the game." Well, I call baloney on the majority of that idiom. Because you have to play the game the right way, and you have to win. What's the point if you don't win?

A little tangent there … back on track to grades and their importance. During every journey, you must periodically check your progress. Is the initial purpose of the journey still correct? Are you still on the right track? Are you on schedule? What adjustments need to be made going forward? Grades capture the snapshot in time of "How am I doing?" Grades enable you to measure yourself and your skill relative to everyone else. Grades fuel the fire for a competitive individual, which is a good thing because the world is a competitive place. Unfortunately, grades are also utilized to stamp a label on an individual. We have all seen it, and if we are honest with ourselves, have fallen into the same trap. Does this sound familiar??

- Pam is a straight A student. She can go to any college she chooses. Her future is a lock.
- Max is a solid C student. He's really average. He obviously will not go college. His future is okay but nothing special.
- Homer is barely passing with just slightly above a D average. Good luck. He's going to need it.

We all understand grades, and hopefully, we can stipulate that my rudimentary depiction of this complex system is acceptable. It is easy to see the conceptual similarities between the system of grades that we grew up with and the performance appraisal process that we utilize in the business environment. The annual performance evaluation has historically been perceived as an employee's right and the organization's responsibility to deliver. Each organization has a different process and utilizes different techniques. However, the basic exercise is extremely similar. There is a performance appraisal form that is completed by the supervisor as well as the employee in the event that a documented self-appraisal is part of the process.

The original creator of the basic performance evaluation form is unknown. However, human resources historians have estimated that this form has been modified and copied more frequently than any other single document template in the past eighty-five years. It is incredible to note that given all the modifications the structural integrity has remained intact. The form has four fundamental evaluation sections:

- performance against objectives
- competency/skills assessment
- job knowledge
- *performance rating*

I have highlighted performance rating because this is where business practice or organizational behavior bears the most striking resemblance to report cards and to the high school experience. Rating schemes vary, but there are generally three to five tiers. Oftentimes the descriptive rating is converted to a number, as outlined below:

1. Marginal
2. Needs improvement
3. Meets expectations or fully qualified
4. Exceeds expectations or very good
5. Consistently exceeds expectations or outstanding

Just like the grades in high school, the performance rating is an identification label that impacts many things in the business environment. The performance rating that an individual receives in the performance-appraisal process is the prime element that generally determines the amount of the base salary merit increase amount or percentage the individual will receive. Oftentimes it determines whether the individual can apply for another role in the organization. It is a key element in being considered for a promotion, and generally, the top-rated performers receive special perks in cash recognition and equity awards. In addition, the performance rating is a primary component in identifying individuals for headcount reductions. Just like grades, the performance rating is a label that defines the individual within the perceived value hierarchy of the organization.

As an example, a rating of meets expectations is perceived negatively by the high flyers in today's workforce because it implies average. A meets expectations rating is defined as "performing all requirements of the role at the expected level of achievement." It is a good rating, but supervisors struggle with delivering that difficult message because they are fearful of losing a person who sees himself or herself as a higher-level contributor. Human resources professionals spend a great deal of time providing counseling to supervisors and employees in the delivery and meaning of this message.

In preparing my notes for this chapter, I was struck by a bolt from the blue when I realized what a complete "goat rodeo" the entire performance appraisal process is in business today. Officially, I will call it the Cirque du Performance Appraisal, and I am sad to disclose that I have been a performing member for the past thirty-five-plus years. I have led performance management training sessions that included topics such as the avoidance of inflammatory and unintended discriminatory language, performance improvement plans, and competency assessments. I have probably read more than ten thousand performance appraisals. I have nagged supervisors, managers, and senior executives to complete their team's appraisals so that we can conduct the performance distribution roll up and finalize the merit increase plan in order to get it approved. The HR team must get that paperwork done. This is a mission-critical process. We robotically went forward with probably the biggest management and organizational time suck ever because we were conditioned to believe that an annual performance evaluation was necessary in order to provide proper feedback to our employees and motivate them to drive higher productivity. In retrospect, it probably accomplished neither.

Supervisors were generally reluctant to deliver tough, albeit accurate feedback because of the probable impact on the performance rating and ultimately, the merit increase and all of the items mentioned earlier. This resulted in rating inflation, which created a serious challenge in how to properly reward the real top performers with merit increases, bonus awards, and even stock options due to the budgetary limitations. For the last fifteen years or so, merit increase budgets averaged in the range of 2.5 to 4.5 percent. With such a small budget, the only way to award a meaningful merit increase for the real top performers was to reduce the amount given to the lower-level contributors or not give any increase, which would result in some very difficult conversations. In the true spirit of "everyone gets a trophy," managers "peanut buttered" (evenly distributed) the merit increases so that all could receive something.

It's the consummate double whammy. Performance ratings were inflated; therefore, employees did not receive accurate performance feedback, and I suspect the real top performers became slightly demotivated by not being properly rewarded compared to individuals who performed at a lower level. This most likely resulted in a productivity decline and possibly turnover. The bottom line is that the primary objectives of the Cirque du Performance Appraisal—providing accurate performance feedback and motivation to achieve higher productivity—were rarely, if ever, accomplished. The time and money spent to fail so badly is just mindboggling.

I stated earlier that I would challenge the concept of a teacher awarding a grade. A student *earns* a grade under the structure defined by the teacher and in my experience, this was an objective framework. At the beginning of the semester, the teacher explains that your grade will be weighted as follows: quizzes 20 percent; exams 40 percent; papers 20 percent; and homework 20 percent, as an example. Whatever the structure or framework, students should know exactly what their grade will be and therefore have no reason to experience the report card surprise. The same expectation should apply in the work place. Individuals should have a clear understanding of the structure in which they will be evaluated and what is expected of them. The individual should be well aware of their performance level, and therefore, have no reason to experience a performance appraisal surprise.

At this juncture, radical reconsideration of these concepts needs to be conducted. It is time that business abandon the grade structure concept that the world of academia utilizes. It is time to abandon the performance appraisal process that relies on the evaluation of skills and competencies resulting in an overall performance rating.

Upon reflection of my thirty-five-plus years as a performer in the cirque, I have come to the conclusion that managers need to understand the relative performance/value of their people assets in order to maximize the ROI of labor costs. In order to accomplish this, we must evaluate individuals on a multidimensional or holistic basis by utilizing weighted criteria that is common to all jobs irrespective of title or salary level.

Everything You Know about Organizational Behavior You Learned in High School

For example:

Name = All Fictitious	Company					
	Organization	Role	Ratings Performance 30% 5 - >110% 4 - >100% - <110% 3 - 100% 2 - >65% - <75% 1 - <65%	Ratings - Job Knowledge Current Position 30% 5 - Meets >90% 4 - Meets 80%-89% 3 - Meets 75%-79% 2 - Meets 70%-74% 1 - Meets <70%	Ratings Potential 20% 5 - Promotable Now 4 - Promotable < 1 year 3 - Good fit now 2 - Reached maximum level 1 - Beyond current level	Ratings Value to Organization 20% 5 - Highest priority to retain long term 4 - Unique skills and key contributor 3 - Critical for current needs, limited longer term 2 - Skills readily available 1 - Not adaptable for future needs	Composite Score
Michaud, Suzanne	Customer Support	Individual	4.0	5.0	5.0	5.0	4.70
Darcy, Ronald	IT	Individual	4.0	5.0	5.0	5.0	4.70
Ramierez, Paul	IT	Individual	4.5	5.0	4.0	5.0	4.65
Jameson, Joan	Marketing	Manager	4.0	5.0	5.0	4.5	4.60
Donahue, John	Sales	Manager	4.5	4.0	5.0	5.0	4.55
Branson, Melanie	Manufacturing	Individual	4.4	4.0	5.0	5.0	4.51
Adai, Joseph	Finance	Individual	3.7	4.0	4.0	4.0	3.90
Sheppard, Greg	R&D	Individual	4.2	4.0	3.0	4.0	3.86
Cooper, Sara	Sales	Individual	4.0	4.0	3.0	4.0	3.80
Yee, Sally	Marketing	Manager	4.0	4.0	3.0	4.0	3.80
Patel, Vinu	Marketing	Individual	3.5	4.0	3.0	4.0	3.65
Wilson, Thomas	R&D	Individual	3.5	3.0	3.0	2.5	3.05
Jackson, Maximillian	Sales	Individual	3.1	3.0	3.0	3.0	3.02

Stack Ranking Tool

The concept of stack ranking in many management circles is strongly resisted. I never understood this visceral reaction, because understanding the relative value of your people assets is the only way to properly reward, motivate, and retain those assets. Every household has a budget. I think it is safe to assume that you are never able to do everything that you would like because of funding limits. So you have to prioritize where you are going to spend in order to get the most bang for the buck. It is the same thing at work. There are limited funds for people, and you have to invest wisely. In all probability, everyone *does not* get a salary increase.

I realize that I am challenging historically fundamental HR practices. For decades, we have conducted this process in pretty much the same manner, with questionable results, in my opinion. In today's highly competitive global business environment, we must be innovative and aggressive in driving productivity and results if we wish to be competitive. We have to push the envelope even further in order to win!

Vic's Fix

- ☐ Shut down the Cirque du Performance Appraisal. It has been a nice run, but it is time for that template to retire. Instead of rating skills and competencies, evaluate and reward accomplishments and results!
- ☐ Stack rank regularly. Know the relative value of your people assets.

- Conduct quarterly business reviews with your team. How are we doing? Are we on the right track? How did we do versus what we said we would do? Where are the gaps? Where do we need to adjust? What are we going to commit to for the upcoming quarter(s)?
- Consider an agile method approach. Accountability to each other is amazing. Good things happen when people are accountable to each other.

4

Superlatives and Employee Recognition

In researching the tradition of selecting the superlatives for high school graduating seniors, I was fascinated to discover that this practice dates back to the Roman Empire circa AD 79. The original distinctions were quite simple such as "most likely to command a Roman legion," "best chariot driver," "most likely to become a senator," or, dreadfully, "most likely to end up in the arena." As civilization progressed, so did our creativity. Today, we have advanced to such arcane awards such as "best celebrity look-alike," "best movie quoter," and my personal favorite, "most likely to put foot in mouth."

Why the superlatives? What do they accomplish? As an underclassperson, I dreamed of my senior year, when I might receive the distinction of "most likely to" or "best ... whatever." I was totally into it until I was not named anything! Then, I thought the whole thing sucked and was just a waste of time. The "cool kids" win again.

Recognition is a performance motivator. Our desire to be recognized for our achievements and contributions has never changed. In fact, a valid argument can be made that the proliferation of social media in the past two decades reinforces that the need is even greater. More than ever before, individuals have a public forum to self-promote and pontificate their views and even banter with celebrities and politicians. There is no barrier to entry for this medium or achievement bar to jump over before you are able to claim your "fifteen minutes of fame." In the not-so-distant past, only significant accomplishment would warrant some form of public recognition. Now, there are segments of our society that seem to value participation and effort equally to achievement and results. Any parent whose children have participated in youth activities in recent years has experienced the "everyone gets a trophy" syndrome.

As you would easily surmise, societal shifts have a significant impact with business organizational behavior. Human resources organizations have been scrambling for years to respond to the need for meaningful employee recognition programs within their respective organizations. The scramble is generally a reaction to a declining employee retention trend, negative exit interview feedback, or feedback from the annual employee survey.

The Futility of Reaction Mode

The human resources team swings into full reaction mode and determines that the employee recognition issue can be addressed with the development and implementation of new human resources programs, as well as reevaluating existing programs. Nothing is better received in organizations than shiny new HR "toys/programs" that are aimed specifically at the employees. The service recognition award program is low-hanging fruit. It is easy to change, and there must be a bazillion vendors that provide this service. After a tedious request for proposal process, a new vendor is selected as our service award provider. We proudly roll out the new program and announce that now we will award you a nice plaque after the completion of your first year of service; a coffee mug after three years of service: a personalized mousepad with photos/press clippings of company events from the year you were hired; and at ten years of service, a Montblanc pen! How cool is that? This will help reduce turnover ... a wicked nice pen!

The HR team is just getting started as they have developed two new programs. The first is a revitalized "employee of the quarter" program, and the second is a new concept called peer-to-peer recognition.

The employee of the quarter program involves a nomination process by the nominee's manager and subsequent approvals up the management chain to the executive sponsor. The nominees will be presented at a special executive staff meeting. The winner is selected based on primarily subjective criteria. The winner is announced at the next all-hands meeting and receives a $200 gift card along with an up-front parking space for the entire quarter. Great program. However, it is a very heavy process with executives doing most of the heavy lifting. The program's life expectancy is eight quarters, tops!

The peer-to-peer recognition program is more in line with the collaborative nature that organizations tend to evolve toward. The agile method is prevalent in technology development functions and is being adopted more in other functions as well.

A key component is individual or peer-to-peer accountability within the team. This program is simple. A colleague outside your department nominates you to receive a gift card in recognition of great teamwork or an over-the-top effort that resulted in the resolution of a problem. The nomination is approved through the two management chains, and the nomination is noted in the nominee's file. Generally, this is considered part of the performance-evaluation process. It's a good program that's well received by the winners. There appears to be an implied quid pro quo where, once recognized, the peer will return the favor. The program is relatively light on process though it requires a great deal of repeat marketing in order to keep it top of mind for busy Individual contributors.

There are many different approaches or programs based on company culture, industry, company size, location, etc. All are good and quite probably result in a positive experience for employees. Recognition programs are an expense. According to Leo Jakobson (Incentive Federation Inc. *Incentive* magazine, July 19, 2016; http://www.incentivemag.com/News/Industry/Incentive-Federation-$90-Billion-Market-Size/), it is estimated that US-based companies spend in the range of $15–$20B annually on cash rewards for non-sales employees. Approximately 80 percent of that spending is for service awards, which leaves $3–$4B for non-sales employee performance-based recognition.

Yikes! Is there another alternative? The answer is *absolutely*. Recognition is not a programmable item. It is a respect and gratitude concept made actionable. I guarantee you do not need to spend beaucoup bucks to achieve it. It is easy to do if you are willing to give of yourself and demonstrate a genuine appreciation and gratitude for your team's contributions.

It is a shout-out in a team meeting or in a scrum for a job well done. It is a morning walk around to get the day started on a positive note. It can be as simple as asking one of your employees how her family is doing. Did they enjoy their vacation? "I know you're working on a critical aspect of this project. How's it going? Can I help you with anything?" Address your people by name at all times, and make sure you pronounce the name correctly. Know that attempts will be greatly appreciated—pizza Fridays, bagel Mondays. Conduct monthly birthday lunches. The list goes on. Employee recognition is about respecting the individual, recognizing his or her value, and appreciating contributions.

Vic's Fix

- Be willing to let your guard down. Show your human side.
- Manage by walking around. Be visible.
- Recognition is important, no matter how small.
- Programs generally have a short shelf life and are usually Ineffective in the long run. Save time and money. Forget the programs.
- Conduct informal listening sessions, such as monthly coffee talks, lunches, or cross-functional round tables.
- Get to know your people. Respect and celebrate them. Honor them!

5

Leadership

Organizational behavior is affected by or the result of many factors and variables. We have discussed several already in the context of high school behaviors that still exist in the business environment. Two factors that are perhaps the most impactful on an organization's behavior are the quality of leadership and the effectiveness of teams. While they do not directly correlate to my fundamental hypothesis that "organizational behavior at all levels is best defined as adolescent," I feel there is value in examining them and discussing opportunities for raising the bar in these critical areas.

Leaders begin to emerge at an early age but really hit their stride in high school. I suspect that is because it really is a leader-needy environment. The National Society of High School Scholars (www.nshss.org), a distinguished academic honor society, reports membership in excess of 1.5 million high school students in 2018. These high academic achievers are already outstanding leaders in their communities. Participation in individual and team sports is at an all-time high for both men and women. In addition to the various sports teams, there is also the band; the cheerleading squad; student government; the school newspaper; the yearbook; the prom committee; the chess club; the science club; the technology club—the list goes on. The point here is that there are many opportunities to step up and be a leader.

In team sports and a few of the other groups mentioned above, team captains are usually selected to fulfill a leadership role and are often selected because they are the top performers. But many others are selected because they have become role models to emulate. They respect the authority of the coaches and teachers. They work hard and practice hard. They give 100 percent effort at all times. They support their teammates and will help a fallen comrade. It is always team first. The best leaders understand that the success of the many is more important than the accomplishments of the one. Good leadership and team success go hand in hand. Teams rarely, if ever, succeed without good leadership. These inexperienced individuals realize either intuitively or though astute observation that effective leaders do it right by setting the bar for other people to reach and then enable and guide them in reaching it.

How is it that fifteen-to-eighteen-year-olds have this leadership thing down? This is a complex question with a simple answer. They are just natural born leaders. I'll share an example from my own experience.

Blast from My Past

When I was sixteen, I was hired for my first real job at the local supermarket. I was assigned to the produce department and was absolutely petrified because I did not know anything about fruits or vegetables. The department was led by a forty-something-year-old department manager, Joe D. (RIP Mr. D). There were two full-time employees, Dick L. and Paul C. The full-time employees did not work any evenings or Sundays according to the collective bargaining agreement in effect at the time. Since the store was open until 9:00 p.m., part-time employees were required to provide coverage. Enter Victor. There were five part-timers in the department. I was number six. Mr. D was always very busy and did not really have the time nor the inclination to teach me the difference between a Red Delicious apple and a McIntosh apple, so I was assigned to shadow fellow part-timer Peter M. so that I could learn the produce business. Peter was two years older than me and was a senior in a private high school in town. I was a sophomore at the public high school.

Peter was incredible. He had been with the company just two years having also started when he was sixteen. He knew everything about the produce department and was well versed on the sales and profitability success criteria. He was truly a leader in the department as he basically assumed responsibility for guiding and mentoring the part-timers. He worked hard and was a quick finisher of tasks. He always did things the right way never cut corners; he was always available to answer our questions. We truly saw Peter as our leader. With no disrespect intended to Mr. D., Peter was *the man*! True leaders are born. It's part of their DNA.

Human resources functions are responsible for the planning, identification, and development of the people resources to meet current and future needs. One of the CEOs that I had the honor of working for described my HR role as "general manager" for the company. He was, of course, making a tongue-in-cheek reference to the role of GM on a professional sports team that is responsible for finding and securing the athletes to build the team. In essence, he was correct. However, as you know, it is much more complex than that. In the sports world, only free agents can select their new employer. Everyone else is contractually bound to their team. In the business environment, everyone is a free agent. This makes building a team and retaining and developing your talented people resources extremely challenging.

Succession Planning

As stated above, the human resources function is responsible for getting the right people in the right role at the right time. The primary focus of this effort is in the identification and development of leaders. Organizations have many labels for this important responsibility. For simplicity, I will use the label of succession planning. This exercise is initially focused on executive-level succession and cascades generally to the level below that or to the director level. The process, in its purest form, is straightforward. Outlined below is the broad framework for an executive succession plan:

- *Conduct assessment of current executive team*—Utilizing the stack ranking tool, illustrated in chapter 3, assess the executive team on current performance, job knowledge/proficiency, current fit/potential, and flight risk/impact assessment.
- *Conduct a skills and capability inventory of current team*—Evaluate skills and capabilities against current needs and future skills needed.
- *Prepare gap analysis*—Identify the gaps that exist with current team and current needs, as well as gaps in future needs. A skill gap example may be the need for cybersecurity background in the R&D organization because there is currently zero expertise. Prepare a specific action plan to address.
- *Identify current backup and readiness timeframe*—Ready Now, 1–2 years or 2–3 years are generally accepted development timeframes.
- *Prepare development plans for internal successors*—Plan should include relevant coursework,

developmental project assignments, or developmental job roles.

- ***Determine which roles or skill gaps will be filled through external recruiting***—This is always a difficult exercise because organizations prefer to solve their problems from the inside rather than go externally. In my experience, roughly 90 percent of the gaps identified can be filled from the inside.
- ***Implement external recruiting plan***—Plan should include sourcing strategy, confidential nature of the search, compensation level, timeframe, and owner.

For the C-level suite (direct reports to the CEO), this process is done almost exclusively with the CEO and the top HR executive. The succession plan for this group is usually presented to the board of directors. The executive team will implement this process for their organizations and the succession plans will be presented to the entire executive team in order to provide cross functional transparency for the identified backups. In many cases, the development plans involve assignments in different organizations

XYZ COMPANY
EXECUTIVE SUCCESSION PLAN
HIGHLY CONFIDENTIAL – CURRENT

Name	Title	Current Assessment	Back-up	Risk Assessment	Action Plan
Kathleen Kahners	VP & CMO	Excellent individual contributor. Not a team builder. Hard on people	Annie Oakley Solid for Prod Mktg role – None for Marketing	High	Begin search and networking process for solid marketing executives with a target need date of April/May
John Dollar	VP NA Sales	Solid in current role. Reached maximum level	Max Commish - Ready in 6 months	Moderate	Schedule Max for executive development courses immediately
Nigel Potter	VP EMEA	Fair rating Not a team player	None	High	Begin search for UK based sales leader with a target need date of January/February t
Sharon Klozer	VP NA Services	Solid in current role.	None	Low	Begin internal candidate identification process. There are no obvious candidates – Network externally –
Homer Pennywise	CFO	Needs to be replaced – Major concern that many key players on the team are at risk	None	Very High	Begin search immediately with a target start date of Nov/Dec

Sample of basic succession plan: XYZ Company Succession Plan

You may have noticed that in describing this process, I intimated a caveat by adding "in its purest form," which means that the assessments and commentary are free from bias and are objective and accurate. Unfortunately, this is not always the case, because we are, after all, dealing with the executive team and the—you guessed it—"inner circle." The majority of senior executives support this aspect of their responsibility. Yet they struggle mightily with the political fallout that could occur resulting from deficiencies that are identified. It is easy to assess the top performers, however, the real purpose of the exercise is to identify gaps and needs as well as to develop a plan to solve those issues. It is obvious that if the deficiencies are softened or understated, the plan will be ineffective.

As an HR professional, I was responsible for coaching the leaders in being "pure" in executing this process. On many occasions, I was more of a negotiator than a coach. As you can imagine, some of the negotiations regarding the inner circle assessments were quite entertaining, although it did not feel that way at the time. Gosh, it seemed like I was back in junior year in Mrs. McDuffie's creative writing class again.

For the organization to thrive, people have to be able to perform the functions as they exist today, and the organization must be prepared for what is needed in the future. This requires leadership and teamwork at the highest levels. This probably means there are people who are fine in today's environment but do not have the skills or ability to perform the role in the future. Tough, tough decisions. True leaders embrace the difficult issues and trust their teams to do their job.

Finding the next generation of leaders by understanding the needs of tomorrow and then, identifying gaps and implementing plans to fill them is the prime directive of this process. Though, in all honesty, this is really an exercise in leadership and functioning as a senior *team*! Leaders are everywhere and at all levels of an organization. Some already have the title that identifies them as such. However, there are many diamonds in the rough. Executing well requires outside the box thinking, true recognition of leadership skills, nontraditional resource utilization, and role definition by the senior leadership team in order to break down the vertical organizational barriers that limit people development.

Blast from My Past

I will explain with an event from my personal experience vault. I provided geographic human resources support for three regions of a company that provided information technology outsourcing services. Since many of the engagements had a significant number of people impacted as a result of the outsourcing event, human resources became a critical element in the proposed solution in the selling process. I became a member of the sales team on these larger engagements in order to provide human resources expertise to the process.

In one particularly huge deal, the sales team was comprised of approximately fifteen individuals from VP to technical support individual contributors. The good news was that we were selected as one of two finalists for the business. The challenging part was that we had exactly one hour to "sharpen our pencil" and shave approximately $800K (10 percent) from our proposal and submit our best and final offer.

The clock was running out. A hasty video conference was organized with urgency to the sales team. The game was on! Interestingly, the first ten minutes of the call were spent complaining about how unfair it was to only have an hour to make such a significant modification to our proposal. At this point, one of the two technical support engineers on the team raised his hand, waiting to be recognized by the team leader, a vice president. He respectfully acknowledged all the comments shared in the first ten minutes and then politely scolded the group for wasting ten minutes of the precious sixty that we had to solve this problem. He went on to say that we can discuss how unfair it was later because we were going to hit the deadline wall in about fifty minutes.

We had two choices. We could walk away from an $8M deal or stop whining, buckle up, and solve the problem. He then went on to take control of the meeting and led the group to a section in the proposal where we could adjust our assumption on service call tickets and achieve the $800K reduction with minimal impact on the gross margin percentage.

We won the deal. It was an incredible event. Leaders always seem to rise to the surface. This particular individual was assigned as the lead technical support individual on the engagement and in three years was promoted to the vice president level. *Bravo!*

Vic's Fix

- True leaders = successful teams = organizational success. Do the math!
- Recognize true leaders and remove the reigns. Encourage them to lead. They exist in every corner of the organization. They are often in hiding because they are hesitant to step into the world of the "cool kids," inner circle, and upwardly hopefuls. Bring them into the light.
- Remember—being a manager and being a leader are two different skill-sets or competencies. I believe a person can be taught how to manage. I do not believe a person can be taught how to lead.
- Encourage leaders to become managers and teach them.
- Embrace the succession planning concept and do it right!

6

Where am I Supposed to Sit?

Have you ever thought much about where you choose to sit in a movie theater? Is it in the middle? Either side? Would you rather be in the back or closer to the front? I am fairly certain that we do not think about it very deeply in the moment. Rather, the choice is most likely made subconsciously because we all have our comfort zones. Where we park our fanny for any activity is an important aspect of our comfort and ability to relax and feel safe.

Our seating preferences are one of many comfort zones that we glide through every day. Others include our morning routine; the route we take to work or school; our favorite Wednesday outfit; pizza Friday; bagel Monday, etc. These routines, habits, and behavioral patterns are developed over time and enable us to feel comfortable and safe. They also make us predictable. I will comment on the downside of predictability later in the chapter. For now, let's focus on butt placement and some thoughts on how we backed into our seating comfort zone.

Seating arrangements in high school were generally established by the class leader or teacher. In the majority of classes, it was open seating though some teachers preferred the alphabetical system because it facilitated taking attendance. My last name starts with B, so I usually sat in the second or third seat in the far left-hand row. This worked out great sometimes because at least one of the perimeter rows was next to the window, enabling me to escape the drudgery of analyzing the outcome of the War of Jenkins' Ear (1739–48) on trading opportunities in the Caribbean. According to Mr. Charles, our teacher of modern European history, this conflict was truly a real *lobal* affair. Seriously? A *lobal* affair? As in ear lobe? Thankfully, I had a window because that line was the high point of the semester. RIP, Mr. C. We liked and respected you much more than the course!

At any rate, whether I was assigned a seat or chose my own, I always sat up front. It had some challenges, because you were in the direct line of site of the teacher, making social endeavors or any mischievous activities severely limited. I must admit that I also chose the up-front seat for self-preservation. It's tough to doze off with the teacher staring at you. In addition to the extra incentive to keep alert, there were advantages that I learned to capitalize on to my benefit. I guess the best way to label it is the "proactively answer the easy questions early" method—or the method. Here is how it works.

While it's been many years since I was in a high school classroom, I suspect the teachers still encourage a great deal of active participation from the students. There are many ways to accomplish this. Usually, the teacher spends the first five to ten minutes of the class reviewing the homework or raising a topic that was conducive to a Q&A format. For the method to be successful, flawless execution was required during this critical first ten minutes. Any action later would greatly reduce the chance for success.

As the teacher struggled to get the students to start their engines, a series of easy lob questions would be offered. The method requires a front seater to vigorously raise his or her hand, almost to the point of being obnoxious, so 1) the teacher notices that the student wants to engage, and 2) if called upon, the student can correctly answer the question, making a deposit in the teacher's "already answered a question" bank. I think you can see where this is going. By answering early, you avoided the inevitable situation where the teacher asks a question and then searches for the unlucky student who has not yet made a contribution. On most occasions, it did not go well for the reluctant student called upon. These were either valuable lessons about being adaptable and maximizing the circumstances to my benefit, or it was purely a matter of self-preservation. In the end, it probably was a little of both. The method, with some slight modifications, is extremely effective in the business environment as well. Go figure.

Internal business meetings fall into three major categories: information sharing/updating, review/approval, and problem solving. It is the problem-solving meeting where the method is most effective because attendees at this type of meeting are expected to offer suggestions or solutions to the problem at hand.

Just like a high school class participation is key and an individual's contributions in such a meeting are generally viewed favorably by the senior people present. The method is perfect in these situations with some modifications applicable to the business environment. Hand waving is not necessary to get anyone's attention. Being prepared gives you the best edge. Contribute early in the meeting before the discussion heads into the weeds and your preparation may not have anticipated the detail. Meeting attendees that do not contribute immediately become vulnerable to the dreaded comment, "You have been very quiet so far. What do you think?" *Bam*! It's the high school class scenario on steroids. Hopefully, you are prepared.

As an observer of the human condition, it always fascinated me how businesspeople selected where they sat in meetings or events. In large group meetings such as all-hands meetings, the back of the room fills up fast. It seems almost planned that the first three rows are almost totally vacant. When queried about why they are sitting in the back, the most common answer was "to keep a low profile." Interesting! Invariably, people were redirected to the front seats, and it was quite evident that they just took a bite out of a lemon. They were clearly outside their seating preference comfort zone.

In smaller, regularly scheduled meetings of perhaps five to fifteen participants, people usually choose the same seat at the table. I felt it was quite surprising how extraordinarily possessive people became regarding their regular seat. Everyone knew where each attendee sat. If by chance a regular attendee's seat was "stolen," a comment was usually forthcoming from the regular seat holder. The comment was made in jest though it was quite evident that the implication was for the usurper to vacate the seat. Occasionally, a newbie would attend the meeting and sit in that seat. The collective gasp could be heard all the way to the cafeteria. Needless to say, the newbie quickly vacated the seat. The boss's chair was always left vacant.

You are probably thinking, *Yeah, right! He's exaggerating because adult business professionals are not that immature.* Actually, they are! I have logged many hours dealing with adolescent behavior in adult business professionals. In this area, it's all about the comfort zone and the belief that you will do your best work from that seat in a particular situation. Quite frankly, I believe the opposite occurs, because when we are in in our comfort zone or stuck in a routine, there is a tendency to be complacent and operate on autopilot. You become less observant of your surroundings. Your actions and thought processes become predictable, making it more difficult to think outside the box and to be creative. This may seem a bit overstated. My emphasis is on falling into comfort zones and routines in general, not just the seating preference.

Does it really make a difference where you sit? Yes. It makes a difference, especially if the table is rectangular. It is clear that there are two distinct power seats at each end. Senior people occupy these seats 98 percent of the time. Interestingly, I have observed that when the two power seats are occupied, the seat holders are oftentimes of dissenting points of view, which makes for excellent corporate theater. A quick story to illustrate the point.

Blast from My Past

The business unit that I supported held biweekly staff meetings with the senior leadership team of the unit. The meetings were scheduled for ninety minutes. The meetings were well organized and managed effectively by the business unit leader to keep to the timeline. The meeting involved about fifteen senior executives and me. I will always recall the first time that I attended this session.

Predictably, all went to their usual seats around the table, with the business unit leader at one end. Since I was a newbie, I was not sure where to sit, so I patiently waited for the seats to fill out before making my selection. As the room filled, I noticed that the seat at the opposite end of the table (the other power seat) was vacant. Strangely enough, the four adjacent seats were vacant as well. I believed that I could safely select one of the vacant four seats without causing an incident. I settled in and established my perimeter with notepad and coffee cup. I was set and raring to go.

Right before the meeting was scheduled to begin, the number-two person in the business unit made a grand entrance and headed toward the end of the table where I was sitting. He selected the other power seat, directly across from the leader.

Once settled, he leaned over to me and whispered, "Are you sure that you want to sit here, rookie?"

I was puzzled by the question and enthusiastically and naively responded, *"Sure!"* What did I know?

He just chuckled as the meeting began.

The meeting progressed smoothly and seemed very productive. The last ten minutes of the agenda was a trip around the table for pertinent brief updates from each functional area. As the updates finally come around to my end of the table, I provided my update. With just the number-two person left, I started collapsing my perimeter in anticipation of exiting quickly to get to my next meeting.

Well, number two launches into a tirade about budgets, headcounts, and how he needs more resources as he was directly challenging his boss in front of the whole team. The slow burn at the other end of the table was building to a crescendo. The tension in the room was as thick as molasses. I had never before seen so many people so interested and focused on their footwear.

The leader exploded at number two for his rant, emphasizing that this type of an issue was not appropriate to be raised in this forum. The leader was laser focused on number two. Then, to my surprise, he turns to me and chastised the entire human resources function for not filling headcount requisitions quickly enough. Just to clarify, this was my second week with the organization. I was then given the action item to schedule a meeting in twenty-four hours to review the status of all the requisitions in number two's organization. The review involved sixty-five openings. I finished the status report two hours before the scheduled meeting.

Upon reflection, I realized that the four seats at the end of the table were intentionally left vacant because number two often antagonized the leader in these sessions. In getting to know number two over the next few months, he admitted that he enjoyed stirring the pot just to keep things interesting. Fortunately, I was able to convince him to try some alternative approaches.

The moral of the story is simple. Be careful where you sit because shrapnel can cause as much damage as a direct hit. Always be aware of your proximity to the target.

Ponder that for a bit and apply the guilty by association concept. It will fall into place.

Just in case you were wondering, my seating preference comfort zone is still up front and to the left.

Vic's Fix

- ☐ When attending an external meeting, seminar, or luncheon, select a table or choose a seat next to a person that you do not know and engage him or her in conversation. Get outside your comfort zone. This is difficult for many professionals, but once mastered, it enhances the learning experience and expands your professional network.
- ☐ For recurring internal meetings, ask your teams to sit in different seats and next to different coworkers in order to disrupt comfort zones. Occasionally change the venue for regularly scheduled meetings.
- ☐ When attending a meeting that includes an individual or individuals who may disagree with you, sit directly across the table in order to address and resolve those differences eye to eye. It is very effective.
- ☐ When attending a problem-solving meetings, be prepared and position yourself visibly front and center.

- Encourage your teams to regularly challenge and question their comfort zones. Push them! People learn best and can accomplish more when they are free from the limitations of their routines.
- Use meeting rooms with round tables as often as possible. It seemed to work well for King Arthur.
- For giggles and grins, check out the War of Jenkins' Ear, 1739–48. Absolutely riveting!

7

The Power of Teams

Collaboration methods and technology tools that facilitate a collaborative approach have dramatically changed how young people are being educated. Group projects are very common, and teams comprised of generally four to eight students are tasked with an objective, and the entire group receives the same grade upon the completion and assessment by the instructor. This approach is almost exclusively used at the graduate level and to a lesser extent at the undergraduate and high school levels. It is becoming more mainstream. This is a positive phenomenon because individuals learn how to function on a team. It bodes well for the business environment, right? Not necessarily.

The power of teams is a critical element that seems to get lost sometimes in the business environment. The word *team* is overused and misunderstood. Sadly, it has become diluted, its true meaning lost.

Most businesses/companies are structured by functional lines of responsibility. A simple structure is sales, customer service and support, development, marketing, finance, and human resources. The leader of each area organizes the workforce into appropriate workgroups within the silo. These smaller groups are often referred to as departments, sections, or teams. Remember—a group of people assigned to work together does not necessarily make them a team regardless of the label used.

Effective teams usually share one common characteristic: unselfishness. It is a simple concept. Each member of the team has a role to perform in order for the team to achieve its goals. Ideally, each function is strategically aligned and successful in order for the organization to exist, thrive, and, most importantly, survive. There is an interdependence on and complete trust in one another. This is the definition of a team.

Many senior business leaders identify with their organizations and are protective of their team and functional responsibility. These leaders fundamentally believe that they are serving the best interests of the organization by doing what is best for their function or silo and oftentimes are not actually acting in the best interests of the overall organization. Therein lies the rub. The challenge for organizations is in reorienting these senior management behaviors to focus on company first. The senior management team must be strategically aligned and speak with one voice. Objectives for each function should be complementary and never conflicting.

High-performing teams are critical to the success of all organizations. How do you build a team? How do you identify team players? How do you build alignments within the team? How do you motivate individuals to perform at their peak capability?

Building a team is kind of like shopping for furniture. You must know exactly what you are looking for, such as dimensions, style, color, material, fabric, and price. If not, it will take forever to find, and in the end, you probably won't be satisfied with your purchase.

The same concept applies to team building. In my opinion, there are a few simple guiding principles.

Building a Team

- **Understand the mission**—Be clear on what needs to be done as well as the skills and resources required to accomplish this.
- **Clearly define the rules of engagement**—This is very important. This establishes the way in which the business of the team will operate and guides how team members will interact with each other.
- **Establish minimum skills standards and stick to them**—Building a team requires basic skill and experience qualifications of the team members.

- **Select a group of qualified individuals with diverse perspectives**—Different perspectives drive better outcomes.
- **Select team-oriented individuals**—Individuals who understand how to be a part of a team and truly function as a team player are extremely valuable to an organization. True team players always put the team first, trust their teammates, support a struggling teammate, never take individual credit, and always describe success in terms of the team's accomplishments. These individuals are driven to perform at the highest level because they are totally committed to their teammates and never want to let them down. This is a huge motivational factor for the individuals on the team.
- **All-stars welcome ... not required**—Selecting the most skilled individual for every position is a plus if he or she is team oriented. However, it does not guarantee success. There are many examples of high-achievement teams that are comprised of well-qualified but not necessarily the best-qualified individuals. I think this expression applies: "The whole is greater than the sum of its parts."
- **Involve team members in the selection process**—Success can often depend on good chemistry between the members of the team.

- **Adhere strictly to the "no jerks" rule**—Self-explanatory and very important! Do not hire them!
- **Establish clear senior management team objectives that are strategically aligned and communicated throughout the organization**—Establish cascading objectives for each department to drive functional alignment.
- **Design bonus/incentive compensation schemes that include a team achievement component as well as an individual performance achievement component**—This encourages cooperation and collaboration within the functions as well as cross- functionally.

A highly functioning team can accomplish great things. There are many examples of this in the sports world. In a business environment, it is a bit more complex because the definition of success has many dimensions. I'll bet you're thinking, *Great. He can't provide an example. We can move on to the next topic!* Not so fast. Here's one.

Blast from My Past

I mentioned earlier that my role in a company was to provide geographic human resources support for three regions of the United States. Each region was comprised of approximately eight to ten branches, with each branch led by a general manager. The GM was responsible for driving sales and profitability. This was a high-technology, fast-paced, high-pressure job.

One particular branch was the second most profitable in the region and ranked number four in revenue. Pretty good performance by any standard. The GM was a seasoned hands-on leader who was well liked and respected by all, especially his team. He demanded excellence from his team, and they worked hard to deliver results. The GM always made certain that the accolades were directed toward the team's members. However, if something went wrong and a storm approached, the GM was holding the umbrella and getting the team to shelter. He protected them when it was needed. The GM and the branch were successful year after year.

Eventually, the demands of the job and his hands-on controlling style began to take a physical toll. He suffered a mild heart attack and recuperated at home for about six weeks. The medical instructions were pretty simple: eat right, exercise every day, and eliminate stress. This was going to be a tall order due to the nature of his job. He and I discussed it at great length before he returned to work. We devised a plan that we thought would work, with our fingers, arms, legs, and eyes all crossed for good luck. The plan was simple to describe but difficult to do. The GM had to relinquish some control and truly delegate involvement and authority to his team. The results absolutely blew us away.

The team took on a whole new personality due to their increased responsibilities and as a result of the trust that the GM afforded them. The sales territories and teams were realigned. Sales team meetings were held weekly instead of monthly. Many other changes brought the team closer together. After two quarters of the new plan, the branch moved up to number one in revenue for the region. The following year, it was the most profitable branch in the company and ranked third in revenue. This team achieved its potential once the leader let go of the reigns.

I am a team person, and I can assure you that there is not a more rewarding feeling than a group of people working together accomplishing great things. It doesn't get any better than that!

Are you a team person?

Vic's Fix

- Get outside your functional silos. Act with the bigger picture in mind. The quality and impact of your decisions will improve.
- Establish a team/company-first mind-set in all activities. Regularly communicate what is going on throughout the company. Keep your employees connected to the world outside the functional silo.
- Hire team oriented individuals. In the selection process, ask the candidate to describe their experience of being part of a team. Listen to how

often the candidate uses the term we versus I. This is the hidden key because it is the individual's natural, unscripted perspective.

☐ Establish team objectives that are aligned with the company objectives, and implement team-oriented incentive plans where payment is earned only when the team objectives are achieved.

☐ Just say *no* to jerks!

8

Yakety-Yak

"**O**h my God! Did you hear about so and so? *No*? Well, wait until you hear *this:* yak-yak… yada-yada, blah-blah-blah"—and the beat goes on! Sound familiar?

According to the Merriam-Webster dictionary, "Information or opinion that is widely disseminated without any *authority* or confirmation of *accuracy*" (emphasis added) is defined as gossip. We have all experienced it in some fashion. Most people probably did not think about it very much at the time, and viewed the "information sharing" as harmless. I've certainly felt that way. The definition is eye-opening: "without authority or confirmation of accuracy." My perspective has changed dramatically over the course of my career because I have discovered that gossip is anything but harmless.

Our society is fascinated by gossip. Gossip is big business, as there are many outlets to satisfy our guilty pleasure. There are magazines, newspapers, social media, tell-all books by insiders, television shows, and my personal favorite, the phenomena of reality TV.

Most individuals get their first taste of gossip candy in high school. For example, in my school the big news in the halls of learning was that Eric and Nicole were going steady. It was all the freshman class could talk about because Eric was a freshman and Nicole was a junior. This was just absolutely scandalous! Eric became an instant legend and hero in the eyes of all the freshmen boys. Eric's exploits were a beacon of hope for us all. The tale reached an entirely new level of drama when Eric's family moved away after first semester. The rumor was that Eric and Nicole maintained a long-distance relationship and that upon graduation, Nicole relocated to be with Eric. They lived happily ever after.

Of course, not a single person could confirm any of these facts. But man was it ever a good story. Interesting observation: the whole class discussed the relationship between these two individuals, yet nothing that happened between them had any impact whatsoever on the lives of anyone in the freshman class. In this situation, we never knew what impact all the gossip had on Eric and Nicole. It is probably safe to assume it had some effect on their relationship.

Gossiping about the love lives of other people is a prevalent form of gossip, and for the most part, it is pretty innocent. In high school, this was probably the most popular topic. It consumed a great deal of lunchtime conversation. I am certain that most people wanted to see their friends in healthy relationships and were genuinely happy that Bill and Betty were dating. So sharing good news was a positive thing. On the other hand, there were some truly not nice people who did not share that perspective. Gossip being what it is—"widely disseminated without authority or confirmation of accuracy"—without any accountability for their actions, these individuals weaponized the gossip as a negative force intended to tarnish reputations or inflict emotional distress. Not so innocent after all!

In the business environment, this human foible to gossip becomes much more impactful and disruptive than the comparatively tame stuff that I referenced at the high school level. Gossip or rumors that may call into question a person's integrity, judgement, fidelity, or character can easily cause harm to his or her career and in many cases, employment. Sadly, being accused is often equal to being considered guilty. Those who perpetuate this type of "weaponry" are well aware of this, and in many cases, they believe that by tearing another person down, they can appear much more capable than they are. It does not get much lower than that.

Despicable right? Absolutely. However, the universe has a way of balancing things out. Justice (karma) is sometimes delivered, although we may not always be there to see it, as evidenced by the following example. But remember—what goes around often comes around.

The high technology industry in the 1980s was absolutely incredible. The Route 128 loop around Boston became known as America's Technology Highway because of the number of tech companies that were started there. The pace was insane. The workload was never ending. From a human resources perspective, turnover was in the 18–22 percent range, primarily because the demand for technology talent was far greater than the supply. People were offered huge raises to jump ship. As a result, merit spending plans were budgeted around 12–15 percent just to have a fighting chance at retaining the key talent. We were hiring people faster than we could get them processed on the payroll. It was just *nuts*, and we enjoyed every minute of the craziness.

If an individual resigned, he or she was immediately walked out. The person's system access was shut down. There would be no company-wide, "Goodbye, everyone. It's been a blast working here, but I got another job that's going to pay me a boat load more money" emails. There would be no going-away parties. It was as if the terminated person was to be stricken from the records and never mentioned again. Companies vigorously defended the standard noncompetition, non-solicitation and confidentiality agreements in order to send a message to the remaining employees. However, success in obtaining a temporary restraining order (TRO) and injunctive relief was very rare in most jurisdictions.

Employee retention was mission critical. Retention initiatives were announced weekly, or so it seemed. Important programs were initiated, such as 401K matching; more generous paid time-off benefits; domestic partner eligibility; and a widespread uplift in benefit levels in general. In addition, senior management wanted to understand the pulse of the organization and listen to employees' issues so they could be addressed and keep people from leaving. Using an approach that was successful in surveying customers, the employee survey, or attitude and climate survey, was born.

The survey was administered by an independent organization and covered areas such as work environment, benefits, your manager, company direction, growth opportunities, and several others. The results were produced in cascading levels, starting with the total company information and then rolling down to each major department. Meetings were held with all the employees in the department where they were presented their department's results compared to the total company results. An action plan to improve issues was to be designed in the meeting. Our company took this process very seriously and acted based on feedback from the employee groups.

Blast from My Past

One fine afternoon on America's Technology Highway, one of our R&D directors was spotted, by one of his direct reports, having lunch at a small, out-of-the-way bistro with a former R&D manager who now worked at our arch rival "the evil empire."

The direct report wondered what they could be talking about. Why were they meeting in such an out-of-the-way place? His brain went into overdrive as he pondered the fact that our company was just about to launch a new product. The timing of this luncheon meeting with our archrival seemed suspicious to him. Now, just hold on, James Bond Jr—your director and his former manager were always good friends. So nah, it was just a social visit. There's nothing to be concerned about—right? James Bond Jr. concluded that since this was our major competitor, it was important to protect us and advise the functional VP of the luncheon meeting. The VP politely listened, thanked him for the intel, and said he would look into it. James Bond Jr. had been totally brushed off.

James Bond Jr. then decided to take matters into his own hands. He asked his boss, the director, what he had done for lunch that day since he was gone from the office for quite a long time. The boss seemed annoyed by the question and explained that he had lunch with an old friend. Even today, I find it hard to believe the downhill chain of events that followed.

Convinced that there was foul play afoot, James Bond Jr. developed a plan to protect the company from whatever his boss had in mind with the *evil empire*. Coincidentally, the attitude and climate survey was being administered in one week. So he contrived a plan to use the survey to get rid of the boss. If the results regarding his leadership and management of the department were bad enough, the company would surely terminate the director. In the five working days that followed, James Bond Jr. reached out to every employee in the department and told them that the director (his boss) was planning major expense cuts that involved a 40 percent reduction in headcount. The only way this could be prevented was to trash their boss on the survey. The gossip gods performed well. The survey results were horrible, and the director was terminated within a week. This action was taken with my full support as a human resources professional. James Bond Jr. was promoted to replace his disgraced boss.

In conducting an exit interview with an individual from that department several months later, I was informed of the scheme. I immediately reached out to the former director and apologized. He appreciated my apology and said things worked out for the best. He had discovered what happened shortly thereafter. But he had moved on. He was truly a class guy. He was not working for the *evil empire*. He told me that the irony of the situation was that he was having lunch with his friend that day to try and recruit him back to the company! If that is not a kick in the pants, I do not know what is.

Just in case you were wondering, James Bond Jr. was terminated eighteen months later for sexual harassment. I handled the human resources investigation and the resulting termination. What goes around comes around.

I have been involved in many company actions such as acquisitions, reorganizations, facility closings, layoffs, and a host of other events that were highly confidential. In many of these actions, the rumor mill was grinding on a narrative about what was going on that was created based on very limited information. Gossip, rumors—it's all the same and it all has the same negative effect within a company because it becomes a huge time and focus distraction for the organization. If rumors are wild enough, they have to be addressed in order to keep things calm. Paradoxically, the mere fact that the rumors are being addressed gives them credibility.

As described earlier, the majority of individuals who gossip prefer to discuss good things about their friends and coworkers. However, there are also mean-spirited individuals who feel just the opposite. This is probably one of the most widespread challenges that organizations face today as it is a fundamental human characteristic. It will never be eliminated. My objective is to offer suggestions on controlling it and minimizing the damages.

Vic's Fix

- ☐ It takes two to tango—and two to gossip. When offered a scoop, or if a conversation starts with a question like "Did you hear about?" just walk away. Do not engage. The tone can be established pretty quickly if there is nobody to gossip with.

- Communicate early and often with your people. Forget the spin. Give it to them straight. Facts and frequent updates are tried and true remedies for "tonguewagginitis." When there are communication gaps, rumors are excellent gap fillers!
- When confidential actions are being planned, identify the individuals that need to be involved to perform the task and bring them into the "circle of trust." Believe it or not, by bringing all the necessary individuals into the circle, a source of leaks is eliminated because the people with all the answers are already involved.
- Shut down gossip and rumors whenever you encounter them. Senior managers, be visible. Walk the floor. It will break down access barriers and eliminate rumors.
- My father gave me advice that I will never forget, and I will pass it along to you. "If you must say something about or to another person, ask yourself the following three question:
  1. Is it true?
  2. Is it necessary?
  3. Is it kind?

"If the answer to all three questions is yes, go full speed ahead. If the answer to any question is no, reevaluate what you were going to say or do not say it at all."

9

BULLIES AND PREDATORS

Bullies and predators have been honing their craft since ancient times. The two labels are often used interchangeably, but there are distinctions. Bullies are typically insecure individuals who intimidate others to make them feel better about themselves. Fortunately, a bully can usually be rehabilitated. Predators, on the other hand, are generally strong-willed, self-centered individuals who intimidate others by fear in order to dominate and control. They are not able to change. A predator is a "bad dude."

What compels a person to intimidate, belittle, humiliate, and possibly even physically harm another person?

Bullies in the Workplace

Unfortunately, this behavior is well known to all of us because throughout our school years, we either witnessed or were the victims of some kind of bullying (and in some cases ... some were the bully). This took many forms, too many to mention, except the relatively recent emergence of cyberbullying. This reaches a whole new level of despicable as technology-enabled collaboration platforms and social media provide people the freedom to communicate their beliefs and opinions without accountability or repercussions. We are all horrified by the tragic events in recent years where some young people have been driven to suicide by this malicious behavior.

Yes, bullying occurs in the business world as well. In some cases, it is very obvious as we observe a manager publicly disciplining a subordinate. We have seen the discrediting of an individual at every opportunity in interactions with others or even going so far as to directly insult an individual. In other cases, the bullying is more subtle, such as failure to include the individual in a critical meeting, withholding information, or not being responsive to requests for information or clarification. These actions are intended to cause some discomfort or stress for an individual. This type of bullying generally comes from the managerial level but can also come from peers or coworkers.

Email is a common medium used to bully and intimidate. Email is a fantastic productivity enhancement tool. Modern business could not operate without it. For all the good things about the tool, it has significantly changed the interpersonal dynamics in the business environment. Many individuals communicate almost exclusively in this manner. Real-time conversations have been replaced by long email chains so that all interactions are documented in what can only be a paper trail for protection. Due to the antiseptic manner in which interactions occur, it is common that you might say something to a person via email that you might not say directly to his or her face. It is shameful that this type of exchange occurs between peers. It is devastating if this occurs between individuals of different levels.

As an independent observer to the drama of the human condition in the workplace, I can confirm that the behavior patterns of avoiding confrontations are predictable and counter-productive. Controversial exchanges, or "email bombs," will often be sent at the end of the business day. The rationale is simple. There is a good chance that the recipient might not see it until the next day. They will return fire in the morning. Following a presumed response-time standard of twenty-four hours, you craft your response. In order to avoid a difficult conversation, individuals will play out this sorry scene. The only way to resolve conflict is to take the high road and deal directly and respectfully with the individuals involved. Do not hide behind an email address!

There are many more examples of bullying in the workplace. Once discovered, it should be addressed and discontinued. Employees are much more aware of bad behavior than many senior managers realize. In organizations, bad news travels fast, and employees are anxious to observe how management will react to bad behavior. If management acts quickly and decisively, they win the battle. If not, the failure to act indicates that the bad behavior is acceptable and even encouraged. Bullying is a challenge in organizations that must be quickly resolved and eliminated. While a bully negatively affects an organization, the bully needs to be disciplined and counseled. Generally, bullies can often be rehabilitated.

There is a far more destructive individual who is active and oftentimes more difficult to flush out: the predator.

Predators in the Workplace

Predators are everywhere, as evidenced by the many horrific events that have occurred around the globe. We live in a world of the twenty-four-hour news cycle. Sadly, we are well aware of the cruelty that exists in our society. Here, I will focus on the type of predator (as it relates to sexual harassment and a hostile work environment) who is likely to be found in the workplace.

The most destructive predators are in the senior management and executive ranks. These individuals are hired into the organization, usually by a member of the senior team. The reference check is clean with a possible indication that the individual is a hard-driving, results-oriented leader who may "break some glass" along the way. The trait is described to be an acceptable side effect as it was necessary to bring about change. This is not seen as a negative by the hiring executive because most executives are hired to drive change or to turn around performance.

The new hire joins the organization with the full support of the senior executive. In the case of the predator, the senior executive sponsor is more of a protector than a supporter. Admitting a hiring mistake at this level is not politically rewarding. So there is a blind spot for at least the first six months. When the senior executive sponsor is presented with negative feedback, it is initially discarded and placed into the category of a transitional adjustment. The human resources team is directed to work with the predator to coach and counsel him or her through their ramp-up period.

The predator is clever and manipulative and reveals his or her true nature almost immediately. Predators use their power and authority to feed their monstrous egos by manipulating individuals in ways that are generally harmful or demeaning. They will prey on vulnerabilities and basic insecurities and manage totally by fear. They have absolute authority over careers and must regularly remind everyone of that authority by frequently demonstrating their power. This usually results in a hostile work environment and can lead to charges of sexual harassment, discriminatory practices, high turnover, and potential civil damages liability.

Predators are not nice people. They are mean spirited and vindictive. They do not care about anything but themselves. They do not care about the organization for any reason other than what they can take from it. In many cases, these individuals are high-energy con artists who convince the people that they report to that they will drive results. They sell up really well and do not give a damn for the people beneath them. They have a spiel that explains away anything that goes wrong in their organization. Unfortunately, before the predator is terminated, the damage to the organization is extensive and far reaching well into the future. There is no place for this person anywhere in society.

Vic's Fix

- Challenge the bullies; they will always back down. Act quickly to adjust the environment that is perpetuating this bad behavior.
- Use email as a communication tool that is intended to facilitate quick updates or respond to basic, noncomplex inquiries.
- Talk to people!
- When the urge hits you to drop an email bomb, step away from the keyboard and reevaluate your response the next day.
- *Immediately remove a predator!* It is better to admit a mistake and correct it than to perpetuate the devastation and destruction caused by the predator.

10

Friendships and Work Relationships

High school is an important and formative period in our lives. It is the bridge between childhood and adulthood, not only in the development of our adult behavior patterns, but in our adult relationships. Many of our lifelong friendships are established during this period of our lives. Unfortunately, we also grow apart from many of our childhood friends. High school is a relationship grinder due to the pressures that arise from the activities you participate in and the individuals associated with those pursuits.

It is natural for relationships to develop between people with shared interests. While researching high school groups, I had to chuckle, because many of the groups have not changed in decades. Here are a few: jocks, brains, hipsters, techies, hippies, geeks, band, cheerleaders, motorheads, skateboarders, and gamers. In high school, the groups develop an almost insular identity where individuals who are not part of the group are often discounted and ignored. As with all things extreme, behavior can occur. Though for the most part, the different groups peacefully coexist within the school.

Friendships are formed that can last a lifetime. These connections arise from shared experiences that bond people together. These experiences can be pleasant or unpleasant. Winning a team championship at any level creates a strong sense of camaraderie and friendship between the members of that team. The accomplishment is obviously celebrated at the moment, and it becomes the foundation for storytelling and reunions for many years to come. Some close friendships probably developed between some members of the team. Relationships formed in pleasant or positive circumstances are easier to obtain and probably, easier to maintain because of the good feelings that define the experience.

On the opposite end of the spectrum, there is the relationship that develops from a shared unpleasant or stressful situation. A relationships that is born out of stress is like the grape vines in Napa Valley, California. You are probably thinking, *What!* I'll explain.

Blast from My Past

A tour of several wineries was scheduled for a recreational activity as part of a senior team meeting that was taking place in Napa Valley, California. Man, I love my job. The tour was very informative about how the vines are cared for and described the impact of the weather and the elements on their fruit. This particular growing season had been extremely hot and arid with virtually no rain. The obvious question from the group was what effect this had on the grapes. The answer was surprising. The harsh elements had a positive impact on the crop that year because distressed vines produce a better grape, which results in a better wine! We didn't see that one coming.

In keeping with the analogy, relationships that result from a shared unpleasant experience probably are closer and more intimate than other relationships. I suspect that the passengers and flight crew of US Airways flight 1549 developed close relationships as a result of their shared experience on January 15, 2009. The flight took off from New York's LaGuardia airport. Shortly after takeoff, both engines were disabled by multiple bird strikes. The pilot, Captain Chesley "Sully" Sullenberger and first officer, Jeffrey Skiles, successfully landed the Airbus 320-214 in what is defined as a "controlled ditching" on the Hudson River, near Manhattan. All 155 people aboard survived and were rescued by nearby boats. The relationships formed with those individuals will remain very strong for the rest of their lives. Whether or not true friendships form is difficult to know.

The Relating Game

Relationships come in all shapes and sizes. Here are a few that we can readily identify with: spousal/significant other, in-laws, parent/child, sibling, friend, professional/ coworker. The list goes on. In this chapter, I would like to highlight two relationship types that are often blended together: the professional/coworker and the friendship relationships.

As in high school, relationships develop in the business environment because of shared experiences. However, the relationship types differ dramatically. High school is an academic environment. There are milestones that need to be achieved such as earning a diploma. However, the majority of interactions during these years are more social than academic. Therefore, the social interactions lead to friendships.

In the business environment, unlike in high school, people are paid to perform a function. Relationships are formed on a professional level in order to accomplish that function. Big distinction! A professional relationship is fairly straightforward in that it is built on respect, co-operation and need. Respect being the key element of a healthy professional relationship.

Workgroups are assembled based on many criteria, such as skill level, experience, and work style or chemistry. As mentioned in chapter 7, team chemistry is an important element of an effective team. It is within this framework that good professional relationships are formed. Remember, in order to perform the function that I am being paid to perform, I need to collaborate and rely on others. Seems pretty straightforward, right? Hardly!

Human nature strikes again, throwing a monkey wrench into my nice, neat definitions. Professional relationships often develop into friendships because we are social creatures. We subconsciously bring the social behavior patterns of our adolescence into the business environment. This is a natural pattern and is generally, a good thing as long as the lines between professional roles and friendship roles are clearly understood. When there is not a clear distinction, problems can occur.

Blast from My Past

I joined an organization, and within a few weeks I observed that every day at 11:45 the same group of twenty coworkers from one department would migrate to the cafeteria for lunch. They would push four or five tables together. They basically had a forty-five-minute party. It became affectionately known as "the corner" and had a striking resemblance to the "football player section" of my high school cafeteria. I visited the corner on many occasions and found that the topics of conversation were about everything except the business challenges of the day. It was totally a social event, and many times it was quite entertaining. This group planned social outings and activities that also involved their families. It was a tight group of coworkers who became close friends. Initially, this closeness produced a strong team that performed well together at work. However, over time, managing the performance of the individuals in the group proved to be difficult because all work-related activities and interactions were shared within the group. The confidentiality of performance and salary-related conversations was not observed. The professional relationships morphed into social relationships, blurring the line between personal and professional interactions. As this example illustrates, it can be challenging when professional coworker relationships become friendships. It can be exponentially more difficult when a manager and a direct-report subordinate are social friends.

Achieving results in business can be difficult. There are many contributing factors to this, such as market conditions, competition, various economic factors, and interpersonal dynamics that exist within the organization. "People issues" oftentimes have to be overcome or worked around in order to get things done. All organizations have challenges in this area because people and organizations will never be perfect. They can be improved by understanding the nature of the relationships and how best to manage the environment in which these relationships develop.

Business organizations are faced with a myriad of problems and challenges on a daily basis that require managers to make decisions on what actions will be implemented. As we have discussed earlier, many of these issues are about people.

How do we identify and retain our key performers? How do we recognize, reward, and evaluate our people?

Who are the future leaders? Who do we assign to a critical task? Who should we hire? Who is not performing? How should we deal with bad actors? How do we build teams? Who do we have to let go? How do we handle salary increases? Recognition awards? Relocations? Layoffs?

These are difficult and complex decisions with many variables that have little to do with the dynamic of friendships within the organization. It is important to emphasize the fact that friendship relationships are always going to develop in the workplace and that these relationships are often times healthy and conducive to effective performance. Therefore, the friendship factor must be considered in order to reach the best decision because it really is the X factor, although it can be a gut-wrenching experience. How difficult would it be to have a termination discussion with your friend? I will take it one step further. How difficult would it be to reach the conclusion that your friend should be terminated?

When professionals become friends, it is important to always respect the professional role of your friend, and never put him or her in a position to have to choose between the friendship and the professional responsibility. This is even more critical in the manager- subordinate relationship.

It would be irresponsible of me to leave you with the impression that social friendships within the workplace should be discouraged. Not true! As mentioned, social friendships will develop and problems can arise.

Awareness is the key element of navigating through those challenges. Many times the awareness of friendships can be leveraged for the benefit of all.

There is a school of thought best illustrated by a famous line from Francis Ford Coppola's classic film *The Godfather:* "It's not personal. It's strictly business." Sounds easy. However, it is difficult for most individuals to be that robotic. I could not disagree more vehemently with the concept because I can confidently affirm that the business of people is *totally* personal. Every action that an organization takes has a personal impact on the employees.

By recognizing and accepting this simple truth, there is only one course of action: to always treat everyone with dignity and respect. That is the bottom line!

Vic's Fix

- Wherever possible, discourage reporting relationships between friends. Emphasize the boundaries that need to be followed regarding confidentiality.
- Set the example for what professional relationships are supposed to be.
- Avoid extensive social interactions and activities that are not business related.
- Establish a work environment that is friendly, comfortable, and focused on business. Lose the March Madness brackets and Super Bowl squares.

- No yakety-yak.
- Establish a no-dating policy for individuals who work in the same department or report to the same manager.

11

Final Examination

The end of a semester in high school was a joyous event in that a break for the holidays or summer vacation and sandy beaches was in view. The conclusion of a semester also proved to be an extremely stressful period because of finals. The exams for each subject covered the material presented during the entire semester and generally represented 30–40 percent of your final grade. Anxiety and stress rolled into one package. Awesome! How well do you remember that experience? What did you learn? How did you apply it to your career?

Many high school experiences that we have explored are analogous to situations in the work environment. Hopefully, you have catalogued the lessons learned from your experiences and applied them. In the case of final exams I suspect that you learned to manage stress. In addition, you probably developed the ability to prioritize the course material for more effective focus on the key elements that would be included in the exam.

In the prior ten chapters, we have delved into many challenges that exist for business leaders in the workplace today: performance management, building teams, identifying future leaders through succession planning, managing work relationships, and employee recognition, to name a few. In each area we journeyed back to high school scenarios and in many cases relived some of my personal experiences in order to identify the same adolescent behavior patterns in your organizations. Acknowledgement and comprehension of the organizational dysfunction caused by these patterns of behavior will enable you to implement the appropriate corrective actions.

I realize that my comments regarding final exams probably triggered some anxiety. However, I can assure you that there will not be a final exam covering the material in the book.

I now offer a summation of the key fixes from each chapter.

Vic's Fix

- Hold people accountable for their performance and the manner in which they perform, and just say *no* to ass kissers.
- Assign titles based on the role and its requirements and match to the market.

- Regularly stack rank. Know the relative value of your people assets.
- Recognition of your employees is important no matter how small.
- True leaders = successful teams = organizational success. Being a manager and being a leader are two different skills or competencies.
- Encourage your teams to regularly challenge and question their comfort zones. Push them! People learn best and can accomplish more when they are free from the limitations of their routines.
- Establish a team/company first mind-set in all activities. Regularly communicate what is going on throughout the company. Keep your employees connected to the world outside of the functional silo.
- When confidential actions are being planned, identify the individuals who need to be involved to perform the task and bring them into the "circle of trust." Believe it or not, by bringing all the necessary individuals into the circle, a source of leaks is eliminated because the people with all the answers are already involved.
- Challenge the bullies, they will always back down. Act quickly to adjust the environment that is perpetuating this bad behavior. Remove a predator immediately.

- Wherever possible, discourage reporting relationships between friends. Emphasize the boundaries that need to be followed regarding confidentiality.

Throughout my professional and personal lives, I have primarily focused on living in the present and planning for the future. I have rarely dwelled on events from the past, other than what I had learned from them so that I would not repeat mistakes. I have, for the most part, been able to put things in the rearview mirror and move forward. You must be wondering why I would spend the time and effort to write a book that is focused so much on my past experiences.

Simply put, I realized the journey back to high school was the most effective method to shine a spotlight on the organizational behavior challenges facing companies today. The more I thought about it, the more I realized that the comparison was one that all could relate to. Recognition of a problem in its true form is the first step on the path to resolution.

So get out your yearbooks. Retrieve those letter jackets and sweaters from the cedar closet, and hang that graduation tassel from the rearview mirror. Now that you have passed the final examination, you are ready to be the adult in the room and lead your organizations to great success. I hope you enjoy the journey!

ABOUT THE AUTHOR

Victor P. Becker earned a bachelor's degree in management from Providence College. He is a retired senior human resources executive with more than thirty-five years of experience in the high-technology and retail supermarket industries. He built a career of experiences in global human resources, labor relations, mergers and acquisitions, organizational development, and talent acquisition. Becker is from the greater Boston area.

CPSIA information can be obtained
at www.ICGtesting.com
Printed in the USA
LVHW090234200819
628263LV00002B/378/P